IT'S TIME TO EAT HOT DOGS

It's Time to Eat HOT DOGS

Walter the Educator

Silent King Books
A WhichHead Entertainment Imprint

Copyright © 2024 by Walter the Educator

All rights reserved. No part of this book may be reproduced in any manner whatsoever without written per- mission except in the case of brief quotations embodied in critical articles and reviews.

First Printing, 2024

Disclaimer

This book is a literary work; the story is not about specific persons, locations, situations, and/or circumstances unless mentioned in a historical context. Any resemblance to real persons, locations, situations, and/or circumstances is coincidental. This book is for entertainment and informational purposes only. The author and publisher offer this information without warranties expressed or implied. No matter the grounds, neither the author nor the publisher will be accountable for any losses, injuries, or other damages caused by the reader's use of this book. The use of this book acknowledges an understanding and acceptance of this disclaimer.

It's Time to Eat HOT DOGS is a collectible early learning book by Walter the Educator suitable for all ages belonging to Walter the Educator's Time to Eat Book Series. Collect more books at WaltertheEducator.com

USE THE EXTRA SPACE TO TAKE NOTES AND DOCUMENT YOUR MEMORIES

HOT DOGS

It's time to eat, the bell has rung,

It's Time to Eat
Hot Dogs

A happy tune is being sung!

What's on the menu, take a peek

Hot dogs today! Oh, what a treat!

The buns are soft, the dogs are warm,

Their yummy smell becomes a storm!

A little ketchup, a swirl of fun,

And mustard lines for everyone.

You hold it close, but don't take a bite,

Wait for the topping, what's just right?

Maybe pickles or onions diced,

Or just plain? All will taste nice!

The hot dog's ready, take a chew,

The flavors dance, so bold, so true.

It's chewy, tasty, oh so neat,

A perfect snack for all to eat!

It's Time to Eat
Hot Dogs

Bite after bite, you munch away,

This tasty treat has made your day.

And when it's gone, you take a sigh,

"Can I have one more? Oh, may I?"

But wait, don't rush, just take your time,

Hot dogs are worth each little rhyme.

Enjoy the fun, enjoy the bite,

Hot dogs make the world feel right!

With friends and family gathered near,

Hot dogs bring the biggest cheer.

A summer snack, or any day,

They brighten up the time to play.

So next time when the hot dogs call,

You'll grab your bun and love it all.

Remember to thank the ones who cook,

It's Time to Eat
Hot Dogs

And take another tasty look.

Hot dogs are more than food to eat,

They're fun and laughter, simply sweet.

So let's all cheer, and shout, "Hooray!

Hot dogs are the best today!"

It's time to clean, the meal is done,

But wasn't that a load of fun?

We'll wash our hands and wipe our face,

It's Time to Eat
Hot Dogs

Hot dog time is a happy place!

ABOUT THE CREATOR

Walter the Educator is one of the pseudonyms for Walter Anderson. Formally educated in Chemistry, Business, and Education, he is an educator, an author, a diverse entrepreneur, and he is the son of a disabled war veteran. "Walter the Educator" shares his time between educating and creating. He holds interests and owns several creative projects that entertain, enlighten, enhance, and educate, hoping to inspire and motivate you. Follow, find new works, and stay up to date with Walter the Educator™ at WaltertheEducator.com

www.ingramcontent.com/pod-product-compliance
Lightning Source LLC
LaVergne TN
LVHW052012060526
838201LV00059B/3999